The Weavers Way
Navajo Profiles

Photographs by Carter Allen • Text by Dodie Allen

Sue & Paul -
You are such a part of my wonderful
1950's memories of Clayton - our
wedding - Evanston. Paul & Carter
are the greatest husbands and our
dear children - We are so lucky!
You get 2 books - a friend's free copy
& the other is our first sale - Thanks
May you & yours always
"Walk in Beauty"
Carter 'n Dodie

Graphic Design by Pam Stone—Day Nite Design
Printing by City Press, Tucson, AZ
Photograph of Carter and Dodie Allen by Tod Martens Photography—Indianapolis
First edition printed 2003

Carter Allen
Tucson, Arizona
(520) 577-2870

ISBN# 0-9655525-2-7

Previous publication by Carter and Dodie Allen
"Cowboys of Santa Cruz County", Tucson, AZ,
1st Edition December 1996
Reprinted 1997
Reprinted 1998
Reprinted 2001

Those of you who have wondered why I have spent half of my life writing about the Navajos can find the answer inside the covers of "The Weavers Way — Navajo Profiles." This is a collection of superb photographs of the Navajo people with excellent revealing text by Carter and Dodie Allen. I highly recommend it!

Tony Hillerman

Tony Hillerman

Best-selling mystery author and proud recipient of the Navajo Tribe's Special Friend Award.

Table of Contents

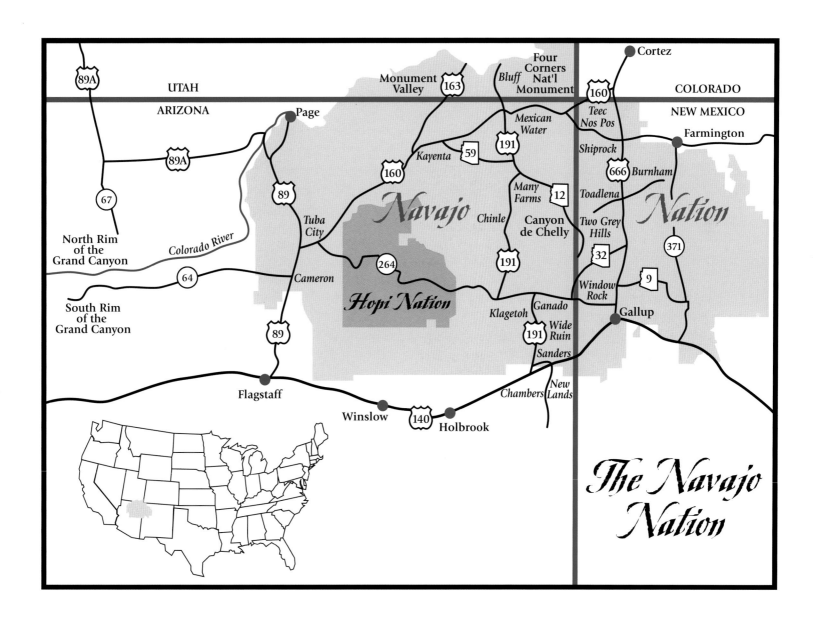

The Navajo Nation

Betty B. Roan

When you step through the worn wooden doors of Hubbell Trading Post, you are surrounded by the past. The floors creak the same song as the old wagons bearing those coming to trade rugs and jewelry over a century ago. You can feel the presence of John Lorenzo Hubbell, friend to presidents, scientists, generals, artists of all fields and—most importantly—the Navajos. Listen as the news of the day is discussed in the softly rolling native tongue. The old stove in the "bull pen" area knows many secrets. The post is still the hub of Ganado, Arizona, much like it was in 1876.

Betty B. Roan is the matriarch of her family and still a stunning lady at 75. She and her husband, Arthur, raised a family of 13 near Klagetoh, Arizona. Her daughter, Emma, has accompanied her to the post on this golden autumn day. Betty learned to weave at her mother's loom and sold a first rug when she was nine. Her wool must be very finely spun to create the tightly woven Wide Ruins and Burntwater designs she favors, using the soft colors of painted mesas and sunset skies. She does

not weave Yei rugs because she believes it "brings a curse on the weavers' eyes." She still keeps sheep and goats for fleece as well as food.

Daughter, Emma, has the gentle beauty of her mother. As the fifth child, she not only helped herd sheep, but cared for her younger siblings. One winter day, she took a baby brother outside and left him sitting in the snow while her mother was at the sheep corrals. She was scolded severely, but to this day this brother rarely wears a coat and loves the cold! Emma went to Greasewood Boarding School when she was six and always wanted to be an athlete. Basketball was her game. Summers were spent near Antelope Lake at the family "sheep camp" where she enjoyed long carefree days. Emma was a teen-ager when she finished her first rug and sold it at the Klagetoh Trading Post for $90. She has been a weaver ever since, as have her four sisters. Now a mother of nine children herself, Emma is proud of her 12-year-old son who has completed his first rug. The Roan weaving talents are legendary and now they move to the next generation.

Bah Yazzie Ashley

Navajo and Emma Spean had six children and all are still living. Their second daughter, Bah Yazzie, is 75 and sits at her loom weaving a Ganado rug. Born between Wide Ruins and Pine Springs, she has always called this area home. The Speans were wealthy with livestock—more than 500 head of sheep plus fields to raise corn, squash, beans and melons. Water was plentiful then. The children were not sent to school because they were needed to tend livestock and help with the farming. Wool has always been a part of Bah's life. She learned to card, spin and dye it from her mother. Emma Spean wove outside, even in the winter snow, because the hogan had no windows for natural light.

When she was 25, Bah Yazzie married John Ashley. She was his second wife. Her cousin, Anna, also was married to him. He had a total of 16 children. All of Bah's children were boys. John died in 1998 and both wives remain good friends. "He was very good to us and treated us well." Today Bah's grandson, Eugene, whom she raised from a baby, lives with her. Her stiff knees have made

walking difficult and a wheel-chair sits in the corner. "The boys" now help her prepare wool and set up her loom. Her soft laugh matches her warm smile.

Bah was always told not to weave Yei rugs—"yeis (deities) are sacred." To avoid danger or bad luck, the weaver must have a ceremony and prayers granting her permission. If a rug has a black border, a spirit line is used so that the mind is not trapped in the design. Prayers from the medicine man also help open the weaver's mind and release her creative spirit. She finds it difficult to weave a special pattern prescribed by a buyer. "It just doesn't work, patterns must take shape in your heart," she says. Bah Yazzie's rugs have won top prizes in important places—the Navajo Nation Fair at Window Rock, Intertribal Ceremonial at Gallup and the O'odham Tash in Casa Grande, Arizona. Her signature is a weaving comb design woven into the corner of each rug. Bah's wooden comb has very short teeth from years of use. She has even re-carved the teeth up into the handle! It has tapped miles of wool into place.

Roy Kady

If there is a "man for all seasons" among contemporary Navajos, Roy Kady might be that man. A well-established male weaver, he is pictured at Teec Nos Pos, Arizona, where beautifully built male and female hogans are used in the local educational programs. Born at Shiprock and raised in the small sheep-herding town of Goat Springs, Roy is a true believer in "Sheep is Life." His mother, Mary K. Clah, is a Master Weaver and the main teacher of Navajo culture to her children. At her side, six children were taught cooking, herbalism, vegetal dyeing and beading as they watched her weave. Babies were propped by the loom in their cradle boards. After elementary schools, the children's paths widened to Albuquerque and Fort Wingate Boarding Schools, followed by Haskell Junior College in Lawrence, Kansas, for young Roy.

The family uses three "sheep camps" for their flocks—Utah in winter, spring near the Carrizo Mountains where they plant their crops, then high up the peaks for cool summer pastures. The brothers loved to have their friends visit the camps for summer vacations. They used the large rams and billy goats as their "Harleys," hanging on to huge horns for a rough ride. Mary warned that they were making her breeding stock "too aggressive." During lambing season, the boys were often "butted" in revenge as they assisted in the corrals.

The children also sold "cedar beads" at the nearby Four Corners Monument, where the boundaries of Utah, Colorado, New Mexico and Arizona meet. Made from Juniper berries gathered from rodent burrows, the cedar beads are boiled for many hours and then strung. The beads are often referred to as "Navajo pearls" and are worn by babies who have not yet laughed or spoken. The beads protect all wearers from evil and bring good luck.

Serious weaving began for Roy in 1985. He received his mother's weaving tools and over the next 10 years, produced rugs of each of the regional styles. There are currently about 16 recognized patterns. Traditional designs are important to him; but now many of his rugs are "story telling, expressions of feeling." Time spent at the loom is spiritual for Roy, who weaves only when he feels inspired. He wants his rugs "to teach the beauty of the universe and the cosmos."

Roy is "Navajo first," but able to comfortably combine both cultures. He is building his flock of the cherished Churro sheep with the help of Dr. Lyle McNeal's Navajo Sheep Project. He also is an avid environmentalist. "Pastures must be rotated, we must return to our agro-pastoral ways," he stresses. Some years ago, his elders declared him a Master Weaver with a Blessing Way ceremony for beauty and harmony. Roy feels he has a gift for teaching and loves a classroom of young people or elders. He is comfortable in front of large crowds or in the solitude of herding sheep. He wants the Navajo to return to their trusted traditional ways and to know the ancient stories and sing the native songs. "The world seems far less threatening when you know who you are," he says. Roy's outlook is broad and contemporary, the old and new woven into the fabric of his 37 years.

Check out his website (www.dinewoven.com) for workshops and tours. "The Navajo rug is no longer just a blanket for wearing or a cover for the floor. It is now an art form to grace your wall," Roy says proudly. Each rug he sells represents a piece of his soul. "I hope my buyers will feel the essence of happiness in my rugs."

Ruby White

Ruby White's weaving career got off to a very rocky start. Both her mother, Eva March, and her maternal grandmother, Louise Tanner, made excellent rugs. Sheep, wool and weaving were in Ruby's blood. The first time she attempted to string warp for a rug was at Red Rock Boarding School on the New Mexico/Arizona line. She used the head rail of her bed as her loom and had to cut the rug off when she was finished. Ruby proudly carried her little striped rug home at vacation time. Her brothers laughed unmercifully at the irregular piece and told her "it isn't even worth a penny." The six year old was so crushed that she hiked far out into the desert from her hogan, dug a hole and buried her little rug. She placed a large rock over the spot, but was never able to locate it again. It would be several years before she wove again.

Ruby continued her education at both Shiprock Boarding School and Intermountain Indian School, always looking forward to summer vacations with her family. The sheep and goats were taken to the "sheep camp" in the Carrizo Mountains where her mother wove under the trees and her grandmother did the carding, spinning and dyeing. Louise Tanner urged her granddaughter to weave. "Don't be lazy like a fly, sitting and rubbing your hands together all day," she would warn. Her second effort brought only $2 at the Beclabito Trading Post, but by age 10, Ruby had completed her first Yei rug. Yei figures face forward and portray the supernatural beings who communicate between the Navajos and

their gods. Now these rugs are a trademark of Ruby White and her only source of income.

Ruby also does Yeibichai rugs with Navajo dancers personifying the deities in profile and with uplifted feet. The figures in both types of rugs are taken from sandpaintings with modifications to preserve the sanctity of the curing ceremonies they are used in. When the rug is on the loom, the figures are horizontal. The weaver must always finish both eyes of a figure before stopping for the day or her vision may be impaired. The eyes are always black and some yeis are hunch-backed. The Shiprock area is noted for Yei and Yeibichai rugs.

Marilyn March Paytiamo, Ruby's sister, and her daughter, Marietta White, are pictured in the Shiprock Trading Post of Jed Foutz. A third sister, Virginia March, is also a weaver. Ruby has been the weaving teacher in this family. "She is our inspiration to create unique rugs," they all agree. It was a brother, Sammy Billy, who suggested they put their initials in their weavings for identification. Ruby also weaves in a "Spirit Trail" or "doorway to let her creative thinking out." Each new design must be a finer weave than the one before. A 3'x 5' rug may take up to six months to complete. Prayers from the Blessing or Beauty Way help keep the weavers' minds centered and open to new ideas. That first buried rug marked the beginning of a most rewarding career for Ruby White. Perhaps Spider Woman took it...

Clara Sherman

Clara Sherman, one of the revered Two Grey Hills area "Grandmothers," sits at the long dining table that is the hub of the historic old Toadlena Trading Post. Clara's velvet-skinned face and soft hands belie her 88 winters in this harsh country. Working with lanolin-rich wool has its benefits! Part of a family of six boys and five girls, only she and a sister remain. Her face is angelic, but her sparkling eyes hint of mischief!

Clara's entire life has evolved around sheep and weaving. As a child, her favorite job was helping with the lambing in the early spring. Her brother, Leo, would take her with him to herd, always mindful of her safety. They would enjoy fresh goat's milk with their picnic lunch. Clara and her favorite sister, Yazzie, hated it when some of the older sheep or new lambs were sold. With broken hearts, they cried along with the ewes at the corrals. Both were anxious to weave, so they would sneak the carding tools and spindles out of the family hogan and practice on pieces of fleece plucked from the barb wire fence.

Clara attended boarding school at Toadlena, which meant leaving her family for much of the year. One spring day she and her friend, Marion, found a dead bird outside the school grounds and decided to perform a fitting funeral. The burial was under some willow trees and the girls found wildflowers to decorate the grave. When they finally heard the school bell, they

knew they would be late. The matron was "very mean" and the girls were not allowed to explain. Marion was crying, but Clara had a plan. That night, they slipped quietly out a side door of the school and ran through the washes by the light of a full moon. When they arrived at Clara's family hogan, several miles away near Newcomb, Arizona, the dogs began to bark. The girls hurried to quiet them as they peeked in a hogan window at her family. Clara feared what her father would say. When Yazzie emerged for a trip to the outhouse, the girls surprised her and there was much hugging and squealing. Once inside, they were scolded by Clara's mother until her father came to their rescue. "Don't speak harshly to them. Give them some of that good hominy from the stove. Let them have a good sleep. Tomorrow I will hitch the horse to the wagon and take them back to school." The lesson Clara learned was, "always speak nicely to anyone in trouble—be a peacemaker." She has always tried to practice this lesson. Clara moved on to boarding school at Fort Wingate, where she was a cheerleader for the basketball team.

Clara's prize-winning Toadlena/Two Grey Hills rugs reflect her strong spirit and determination. She feeds her sheep corn and hay each day and the quality of her fleece reflects it. She uses a Spirit Trail in her weaving "to let all (her) creative energy out for the next rug." Her designs come from her head and her heart and flow through her soft, supple fingers.

Brenda Spencer

When Brenda Spencer enters the venerable old Hubbell Trading Post in Ganado, Arizona, she is like a breath of fresh spring air. Her face glows with a warm smile and her eyes sparkle with confidence. This is the place she has worked since 1983. She is the right hand and assistant to manager, Bill Malone. Her first job here was weaving in the Visitors Center. The post was founded by John Lorenzo Hubbell around 1878 and was operated by his family until it was sold to the National Park Service in the late 1960s. Hubbell was known as the dean of traders to the Navajo. Honest in his business dealings, he was a trusted friend and guide to the white man's world.

Brenda was born into a weaving family. Her mother, Marjorie, and grandmother, Mamie Burnside, made excellent rugs, but did not push her or her three sisters to weave. Childhood was a time to play and attend school. Elementary grades were in Wide Ruins followed by boarding school in Holbrook, Arizona. Then Brenda was chosen for a placement program that sent her to Salt Lake City, Utah, where she graduated from high school. Always known as the "impatient one" in the family, Marjorie was sure "weaving would be too dull

for Brenda. She "put up" her first rug when she was 20. She sold it to Hubbell for between $250 and $300 and Brenda's career took off.

Weaving has enlarged her world far beyond the reservation. She often travels to shows around the country to discuss and explain Navajo weaving. She favors the regional styles of Burnt Water and Wide Ruins, using commercially processed wool of earth and sunset pastels. While traveling, she envisions new designs in her mind, using colors that fit her moods. Other weavers inspire her as they exchange ideas in seminars. Brenda finds great pleasure in her work and is happy to sell her rugs so others might enjoy them. It would "be greedy to keep them for yourself." During the weaving process she is "relaxed, just letting the pattern develop."

There is never enough time. Hubbell is a full-time job and she is also the mother of a teen-age daughter and an eight-year-old son. If her daughter follows in the footsteps of her grandmother, mother and aunts, it must be her decision. Brenda's future is bright. Her rugs bring her "much joy" and she will "follow the path where weaving leads."

Evelyn George

The home of Evelyn George and her husband, Henry, is situated among large trees down the road from the "Benally compound" (pg 23). Evelyn and Lee Benally are clan brother and sister. There is a large barn where Henry works on farm equipment and several out buildings on the place. Everything is very tidy, reflecting the care of the lady of the house. The peace and beauty in Evelyn's sweet smile must come from a contented heart. Her intricate designs show her love and devotion to a life of weaving.

Evelyn began the road to the loom by working with the sheep in the corrals. Her great-grandmother showed her how to tend to the new-born lambs—drying them and protecting them from being stepped on until they were steady on their feet. She remembers checking the sheep at night with only a candle to light the way. As she grew older, she was allowed to help with shearing, eventually being taught to clean the fleece, card and finally spin it into yarn. Weaving was a family enterprise. She learned to cook and sew while attending school through the fifth grade, but then was needed by her family.

The first rug that Evelyn completed was a striped one. She gave it to her aunt as a thank you for helping her. She was about 15, a typical age for young Navajo girls to pass through puberty and be allowed to "put up a rug." Her first spindle was made from a tin can. The geometric designs that appear from her nimble fingers represent clouds, crosses, lassos and sandstone. All are her interpretations of her surroundings. The "spirit trail" she weaves in before she finishes each rug, allows her to have an "open heart and creative mind" for the next fine textile.

Her marriage to Henry was "arranged," which was common in her generation. It was his great-grandmother who became concerned that he spent all his time caring for family, horses and sheep. If a young man did not take time to attend the "squaw dances," how could he ever find a wife? Led by the matriarch, the George family called on Evelyn's family hogan to discuss the details of the matter. For the ceremony, Evelyn and Henry ate cornmeal mush from the four corners of a wedding basket and "in the Navajo way" were married. That was some 40 years ago and Evelyn still smiles when she remembers the day.

Evelyn's daughters, Dorothy and Emily, have increased the family to include six grandchildren. One granddaughter, Natannii, is a college student in Gallup, New Mexico. She has inherited Evelyn's natural beauty, and hopefully, the magic of her weaving.

Marie Begay

Marie Begay has just delivered a mound of wool to the Burnham Trading Post in Sanders, Arizona. She is the "color magician" of vegetal dyeing. Her skeins of wool supply local Navajos, other trading posts and weavers as far away as Germany, Australia and Hawaii with a rainbow of colors.

Marie is a happy person with a warm, engaging smile that hides her 58 years. Her grandmother, Nadesbah Descheenie, took over her care when she was only 8 weeks old, feeding her goat's milk, and raising her along with her cousin, Jimmy. Grandma taught her that "sheep is life—they supply both clothes and food and provide security for the people." Grandma's flock of 500 head kept her and the young ones busy herding, shearing, washing, carding and spinning. Half of the wool was kept for weaving and the rest loaded on the wagon for sale to the surrounding trading posts. Marie learned to weave from her grandmother. Her first striped rug, about 3'x7' and slightly hour-glassed, brought $78 from the Pine Springs Trading Post. Marie remembers feeling great pride as she bought candy, socks and tennis shoes. Her next rug was much improved, and although it was smaller, the price was $350.

Roy and Marie Begay have been married for 36 years and are the parents of eight children—five daughters and three sons, who have produced 27 grandchildren. This close family loves to gather on weekends at their "sheep camp" near Klagetoh, Arizona, to share food and lots of jokes. Her sons

help haul the water and wood for the dyeing vats.

To prepare herself for the day of work, Marie greets the dawn with morning prayers and a handful of corn pollen. The door of a Navajo home always faces east. "The prayers enable me to do a good job—produce rich and consistent colors," she adds. Plants and berries are gathered in June and July and dried for later use. Even rusty tin cans sometimes enter into the mix. The water must be boiling hot for even color. Batches of 10 to 60 skeins are placed in the dye and left for minutes to hours depending on the desired depth of color. The wool is then rinsed two times and hung from shade trees to dry. Marie never dyes on a cloudy day. "There must be sun for good results," she says. Husband Roy, is the silent type, but always a help mate with the wool. Marie says that "his pants and shoes will be out the door if he doesn't." This threat is followed by a big smile!

Marie also finds time to create marvelous rugs. Ganado designs with the trademark red are her favorites. She keeps herself in shape by jogging early in the morning. "Lazy" is a bad word to her. Grandma lived to be 107, so longevity is in her genes. She also knows that she can count on her children, especially daughter, Patricia Ann, to continue her work. When asked about some of her dye recipes, the answer sounded much like, "If I tell you, I must kill you." Worry not Marie, your secrets are safe!

Geneva Scott Shabi

Another of Marjorie Spencer's daughters is the talented and attractive Geneva Scott Shabi. She has fond memories of playing school with her three sisters. They also made pets of the lambs and kid goats that they cared for. Geneva remembers wanting to be a beautician, so her sisters became her "guinea pigs." They endured some wild and crazy hairdos!

Geneva attended high school in Holbrook, Arizona, where she became interested in accounting. She uses that skill now in her part-time job. Weaving started when she was 12. Mom helped her "put up a rug", but was sure that she would "give up before she was finished." She shocked everyone by completing a 2'x3' Wide Ruins rug and selling it at the Hubbell Trading Post. Today weaving is still her passion.

After high school, Geneva married and had five children. Her only daughter, Celesly, was featured as a weaver in a '93 *Arizona Highways* issue. Today she is busy with two daughters of her own, but Geneva is hopeful that she will get back to creating rugs. This family favors the vegetal-dyed commercial wools, but on occasion will re-dye to obtain a special color. Geneva still makes Wide Ruins designs, sometimes with the Two Grey Hills earth tone colors or some Ganado Red for a different effect. In 1995, she won Best of Show at the prestigious Gallup Intertribal Ceremonial Show in New Mexico. This award joined numerous other first places.

Her grandmother, Mamie Burnside, was her favorite person and a "real character." Geneva fondly remembers long summer evenings when the sisters sat outside with Grandma and talked into the night. She taught them to be "ladies." They all miss Mamie!

Angie Silentman

The "home site lease" of Clara Sherman lies down a web of rutted roads in sight of the Two Grey Hills, the mecca of fine weaving. The compound includes several hogans and the house of Angie Silentman, Clara's daughter. Not only are sheep at home here, but dogs, cats, rabbits and a llama share the high desert space. Angie also is a weaver, taught by her mother and Aunt Yazzie, both masters of the craft.

Angie remembers making off with the carders and spindle on occasion to practice on her own. When she would return home from school at Toadlena, she did her chores quickly and waited for her mother to leave on an errand. Seated at Clara's loom, she would pull out several strands and then reweave them. Later, by the light of the Coleman lamp, Clara was well aware of her daughter's intrusion. "If you want to learn to weave, just ask me, but leave my rug alone!" she would say. Around 14, Angie was "putting up" her own rug.

Each summer, the family moves the sheep to the cool green pastures of the Chuska Mountains. There they find fresh grasses and some relief from the heat. Weaving is done under the Juniper trees on smaller looms hung from the branches. This is a relaxing time to be together and share ideas. Angie tried

drawing a rug pattern once. As she began to weave, she put the paper aside. "The finished product was in no way like my sketch." In the Navajo way, the design is within the heart.

Angie is the heir apparent of her mother's herd of sheep—some of the finest in this special area. Little dyeing of wool is necessary here because the earth tones—beige, gray, taupe, brown, white and black—of the Toadlena/Two Grey Hills designs are represented in the colors of the flock. The family selects its own fleece first and sells any remaining wool. Angie remembers the excitement when her mother would finish a large rug. The kids would do the household chores quickly and willingly, knowing the rug money would buy them many goodies.

Following Navajo tradition, families take care of their own. When Clara's favorite sister, Yazzie, was disabled by a stroke, Angie remembers riding her bike to her neighboring hogan daily to deliver food and offer comfort. Today she is the mother of two girls and two boys. Her 22-year-old daughter, Arlana, also weaves and youngest son, Adriano, was only five when he wove a difficult sash belt in the Head Start program. The tradition is strong—weaving will prevail.

Rose Blueeyes

When Rose Blueeyes thinks about her childhood and learning to weave, she thinks about her Nali (her father's mother), Elsie Lewis, now 88. Like many Navajos, her happiest memories revolve around her grandparents. Grandfather would tell stories during the long winter nights and Grandmother was her weaving mentor. Unlike today with her own sons, there was little for a child to do inside— no television, CDs or electronic games. Her father had sheep and the tools of the trade were readily available. Summertime meant "sheep camps" in the mountains with Grandpa and a brother or two. She learned to card, spin and weave in the cool shade of the pine trees.

Rose was born in Shiprock, New Mexico, and went to boarding school at Sanostee. She liked the food, a diet more varied than at home She could go home on weekends and she enjoyed the school activities, especially volleyball. Being the only girl in a family of five brothers, she loved having girl friends.

Her first rug was a small one, which she still treasures. Today, her work consists of very intricate geometric designs with little negative space, woven in the Toadlena/Two Grey Hills style. She can do all phases of the weaving process—shearing, washing, carding, spinning and set up. It may take months

to be ready to weave. Rose has used some commercial yarns in the past, but credits trader Mark Winter with her return to the old ways. Mark came to Toadlena Trading Post in 1997 and re-established it. The "rug room" there is a museum. He has written the genealogies of over 30 prime weaving families with Rose Blueeyes' help. The rugs are displayed in family groupings in a marvelous show called, *Generations*. Rose is photographed with her family display, her rug is top and center. She also was anxious to include her mother, Margaret, and grandmother, Elsie, in a photograph.

Rose married Freddy Blueeyes when she was 23, and they have two sons. The boys, at 11 and 13, sold their rugs for the family collection. Because of her weaving, Rose's world extends to gallery shows, Santa Fe markets and Ceremonials to help educate people on the fine points of Navajo weaving. When the eye is trained to distinguish real quality, the worth of a rug is easy to understand. "Grandmother" Virginia Deal, (pg 25), is a weaver of tapestries and an inspiration to Rose. Virginia spun a ball of very fine warp and presented it to Rose. "It was the nicest thing anyone could have given me," she said. Tapestry quality begins with 80 wefts to the inch, and can exceed 120. This is truly museum quality and Rose welcomes the challenge.

Emma Benally

Hogans are the traditional habitat of the Navajo people. The older versions were made with three forked poles as the main support forming a cone-shaped top and were known as "male hogans." Most of these have been replaced by the more spacious six-or-eight sided "female" varieties with a domed top. They can be made of adobe, stone, logs or wood frame. Most have a smoke hole in the middle and the door always opens to the east. It is customary for the Navajo to greet the dawn with a pinch of corn pollen to bless the day. At the Benally compound, a new nearly finished hogan, consists of only one room. This is the place where Emma weaves. Each family, regardless of more modern dwellings, usually has a hogan for ceremonial purposes, if not to live in.

Emma is 63, the mother of nine and grandmother to 14. Six of her daughters weave. She had to leave school when she was 10, to help her ill mother and take care of a little brother. Both her grandmother, Daisy Hoskie, and her mother, Mary Jolly, taught her to weave when she was about 17. She remembers

selling her first rug to the Shiprock Trading Post for $45—$20 in cash and $25 in credit for groceries. The trading post was the center of commerce for the Navajo, supplying the needs of the family, along with gossip and news. Emma's life is much more mobile now, but she will still weave for three to four hours at a time sitting on the hogan floor. Her finished rug will be sold at the Toadlena Trading Post and the price could be five figures.

When Emma was 17, she met Lee Benally at the Newcomb School, where she worked in the kitchen. He was visiting his brother, who was a Navajo policeman. They wed in 1957. Lee is a real handyman and has a "hogan industry" fixing all types of machinery and cars. He also makes spinning machines. Using the bottom of an old treadle sewing machine, he fashions a foot-powered spinning wheel. His clan sister, Evelyn George (pg 13), lives a short walk away and also has one of his inventions.

Virginia Deal

From the top of the ridge behind Virginia Deal's hogan, there is a clear view of the Two Grey Hills. These hills, as well as the surrounding mesas and valleys, have become a hallmark area of Navajo weaving excellence. Using the various earth tones found in the fine flocks of sheep, there is little need to dye the fleece. The quality of this local wool is quite distinctive and can be very finely spun. At 76, Virginia is certainly one of the premier weavers of the legendary Toadlena/Two Grey Hills style.

She is the oldest of 11 children in the family of John and Maxine Cohoe. She grew up as somewhat of a tomboy, close to her father and the proud owner of a white-faced donkey named "Nipple". This dear pet was her transportation and the means of escaping tasks her mother had for her. She liked to herd sheep and used the donkey to move the flocks to summer pastures in the Chuska Mountains. She attended Toadlena Boarding School for a few years and learned to be an accomplished seamstress.

Virginia's first weaving experiences were alone at her mother's loom. Her mistakes were always noticed and she was scolded frequently. Finally at 13, she got to "put her own rug up." The finished product was far from perfect, but George Bloomfield at Toadlena Trading Post paid her $16 for it. Her outstanding career had begun.

Tapestry weaving requires multiple spinning for the finest yarns to achieve 80 to 120 wefts per inch. All of Virginia Deals' textiles are tapestry quality and are eagerly sought after by collectors. She was awarded Best of Show in 1999 at the prestigious Inter-Tribal Ceremonial Show in Gallup, New Mexico. A buyer once stopped at her hogan when she was nearly finished with a rug. When he inquired about the price, she told him that she wanted a pickup truck. Several days later, he returned to tell her that her truck was waiting in Gallup, New Mexico. Her brother drove her down to pick up the wintergreen-colored vehicle. Both buyer and seller were very happy. Virginia and her truck were featured in the July 1974 issue of *Arizona Highways* magazine.

Virginia has five girls and five boys, including one set of twins. Her skin glows like the crushed velvet of her blouse and her smile is enchanting. A visiting grandson calls her "beautiful." On a recent trip to Indian Market in Santa Fe, she stayed in the home of Toadlena Trader Mark Winter and his wife, Lerin. She was promised breakfast in bed and when asked when she usually awoke, Virginia said quietly, "4 a.m." Breakfast was served on time. Life styles may have changed somewhat for Virginia, but her Toadlena/Two Grey Hills weavings remain masterpieces!

Mary Kee & Racheal

Mary Kee represents a generation of Baby Boomer weavers. She is a busy mom with four children and a full-time job with the Ganado school system in the Human Resource Department. Evening hours and summers find her at her loom producing rugs with Ganado Red, shades of gray, taupe and black. In 1998, one of her rugs was featured in *Arizona Highways* magazine. Weaving to her is an "expression of self. "Designs emerge from her "head and heart and come to life through (her) fingers."

Born to Richard and Ellen Billie, Mary grew up and went to school through the eighth grade in Greasewood. She went to high school in Ganado, Arizona. She loved to be outside and worked with her father tending the sheep, cattle and horses. Herding became a real treat when a motorcycle entered the picture. Mary had a pet goat that she called, "tl izi." One day after separating the sheep, the goat refused to follow her home. Frustrated, she began to peel an orange and leave a trail of pieces behind her. The little kid followed the orange parts all the way home, just like "Mary Had a Little Lamb."

Both her mother and maternal grandmother, Lucy Lee, taught Mary to weave. Her first rug was striped, made from various colors of leftover yarn. After Mary's first child was born, her mother-in-law helped her begin to weave rugs to sell. She sold it for $15 in trade at the Sunrise Trading Post. Grandmother Lucy is in her late 80s and now resides in a nursing home in Winslow. She taught herself to weave with one hand after suffering a serious stroke.

Pictured with Mary is her daughter, Racheal, a recent graduate of Ganado High School. She works part-time at the Hubbell Trading Post in Ganado. Racheal began college at Eastern Utah (San Juan Campus) in Blanding, Utah, in August of 2002. She also weaves, learning by watching her mom at the loom. Dad, Leon, is picking up the art as well. After all, as little sister Stephanie says, "It's easy, you just go up and down and up and down", tapping the weaving comb!

Priscilla Sagg

The Great Navajo Reservation stretches northeast of Monument Valley into Utah. Just across the San Juan River is the town of Bluff and a delightful trading post run by the Simpson family. Duke Simpson began trading in the 1940s and built Twin Rocks Trading Post in 1989. Nestled under the massive red rock towers, the post is easy to find and a great place to shop.

Priscilla Sagg has worked for the Simpsons for 13 years. She lives south of Bluff in the Boundary Butte area. The "Yellowman Family Compound" is near Rabbit's Ear Rock. Every direction offers a vista of red rocks and cobalt skies. Priscilla was born in her family hogan in a place that means "where the rocks end." Her family of 10 girls provided plenty of playmates and eventually five weavers. The children herded the sheep and goats. The girls offered unlimited babysitting for the younger ones. They used to dress in their mother Gladys Yellowman's clothes when left alone and feed the babies from the bottle. Toys were few, so the sisters made dolls out of petrified wood pieces and dressed them in homemade clothes.

Schooling included Tees Nos Pos and Dennehotso Boarding Schools in Arizona, followed by middle school at Mexican Hat, Utah. Priscilla went on to attend San Juan High School in Blanding, Utah. Her weaving education was acquired by watching her mother and older sisters at the loom. She wove her first little rug when she was 12 and a sister still has it. When Priscilla is really famous, it may be worth a lot of money.

Priscilla met her husband, Luke, when she was working at the Mexican Water Trading Post. They are the parents of three sons and one daughter. With the children nearly grown, they enjoy the rodeo circuit, where Luke ropes steers for the United States Team Rodeo Championships. There is still plenty of time to weave and Priscilla's favorite designs are Two Grey Hills and Eye Dazzlers. Her grandmother, Mamie Howard, lived to be 105. She would warn Priscilla that weaving tools were to be used for weaving only. Never discipline a child with a comb or batten. "If you leave a batten in your rug, an ancestor will come and weave," she said. Mamie may be awaiting her chance!

Mary R. Baldwin & Mae Jean Chester

Behind the Hubbell Trading Post is the home of the famed trader, Lorenzo Hubbell. The son of a "Connecticut Yankee," he married into a family of Spanish descent and began trading in Ganado, Arizona, in 1876. Tours of the homestead are conducted daily by the National Parks Service. Hubbell entertained presidents, generals, writers, scientists and artists from around the globe. Today, Mary R. Baldwin and her daughter, Mae Jean Chester, have stopped by to trade. The post still operates in the traditional way as a market for rugs, jewelry and baskets and as a source of foodstuffs and household supplies for the Navajo.

Mary Baldwin's first small rug brought only 50 cents from a trader at Greasewood, Arizona, when she was nine. Her mother and an aunt, Mary Bitsilly, have been her weaving mentors. She found herself a single mom with nine children at home when her husband, Francis, died more than 20 years ago. Mary was able to support her large family by selling rugs, working at the "chapter house," the local Navajo headquarters, and for the Bureau of Indian Affairs. All of her five daughter are weavers, as well as several of her daughters-in-law. Besides weaving Ganado Reds and Klagetohs, Mary has done Burnt Water, Wide Ruins and Eye Dazzler patterns. A tragic house fire destroyed a Sandpainting rug that was nearly finished on her loom.

Daughter, Mae Chester, has 10 children of her own, six boys and four girls ranging in age from 21 to a baby of 1 year. She remembers working at Mary's loom and making "many mistakes" before she had her own rug "put up." The family dog made off with her first loom. The Baldwin kids loved to play basketball and baseball. They also found plenty of ways to get into trouble. Mae remembers hiding all the men's clothes one day when they were in the sweathouse on the hill!

The family loves to gather at its compound for holidays and birthdays. When Mary was asked how many grandchildren she had, her answer was "a lot!". The final count was 33 and one great-grandson. Mary always cooks their favorite "turkey", along with plenty of mutton. Everyone pitches in to complete the meal. Weaving has been good to the Baldwin family and, at age 68, Mary still produces best sellers from her loom.

Mary Henderson Begay

Hubbell Trading Post, one mile west of Ganado, Arizona, is a National Historic Site and administered by the National Park Service. A short walk from the 1876 old stone post is the building housing the Visitors Center. On this day, Mary Henderson Begay sits at her loom creating one of her masterpieces. She shares a soft laugh with an interested tourist. Her gentle beauty and warm smile draw everyone's attention. On one occasion, an eager customer was so bedazzled with the striking lady that he wanted to take Mary home. To prove his intentions, he had his credit card ready!

Mary is the daughter of Grace Henderson, a highly respected weaver herself. When Mary made too many mistakes at her mother's loom, Grace "put a rug up" for her. She was only six years old. Today, she is a full-time employee of Hubbell, weaving most of the regional designs. She likes to change patterns to keep her creative mind fresh. A very complicated Teec Nos Pos design

might be followed by a flowing Burntwater or a Crystal. She does not do Yei or Sandpainting rugs because of Navajo myths that warn of bad luck. Her finished works bear her initials and the date. This seems to be a "Hubbell thing," but is a great idea for the buyer.

If Mary had been able to go to school, she would have studied nursing so she could work in a hospital. Instead, she became a homemaker and the mother of five children. Her two daughters are also weavers and she plans to work with her granddaughters when they are older.

Mary feels the quality of most Navajo weaving today is excellent. Traders such as Bill Malone have helped the weavers get fair prices for their work. Because of her exposure to the public, Mary gets special orders from many of her satisfied customers. Though the work is tedious with a small rug often taking months to complete, Mary feels the future looks bright. "You cannot be lazy," she warns.

Barbera Teller Ornelas

Barbara Teller Ornelas chose to be born on Thanksgiving Day. She entered this world a bit early and surprised her parents, Sam and Ruth, as they were gathering pinon nuts near Montrose, Colorado. After the birth, the baby was swaddled in blankets and the nut harvest was completed before the family returned to New Mexico. Perhaps this shaped the destiny of the tiny baby girl—determined and confident with a strong sense of self.

Barbara joined an older sister and brother, later becoming the middle child after the addition of a younger brother and sister. The Teller siblings were each others best friends, "a group", taught to be loyal and dependable to each other. The family lived behind the Two Grey Hills Trading Post where Sam Teller worked as a trader for 32 years. Ruth demonstrated weaving to a constant flow of tourists. The trading post life afforded the children insight into the outside world and broadened their early educations at Toadlena Boarding School. Weaving was a family tradition. Both grandmothers, Nellie Teller and Susie Tom, made sure the girls learned the craft. Barbara completed her first rug when she was eight, but she wasn't an eager student. She shared her father's love of cowboy movies and once told her grandmother that she planned "to go to Hollywood and be a star." Her first rug, somewhat hour-glassed, is back in her collection after she found it much later, under her brother while he worked on his car.

Following graduation from Toadlena, Barbara went on to junior and senior high school in Aztec, New Mexico. It was a public school with boarding facilities for Navajo students. Holidays and vacations were spent with her family, but her world was becoming ever larger. Her parents were Christians, so many Navajo myths and legends were not taught. To her, weaving has "spiritual value." She has great respect for the loom and the wool and would never attempt to weave when angry. Barbara sees patterns in all aspects of life and this helps her form designs. She incorporates a "weaver's path" in her rugs to "promote harmony and free the creative spirit."

Barbara's next move was to Phoenix, Arizona, where she attended business college. There she met David Ornelas, who was studying at Arizona State University in Tempe. After they married, he encouraged her craft. Weaving became a main source of income while David completed a pharmacy degree at the University of Arizona in Tucson. The family continues to live in the city. Their son, Michael, and daughter, Sierra, represent the next generation of weavers.

Elder sister, Rose Ann Lee, and Barbara completed a 5'x8'10" Two Grey Hills tapestry that won Best of Show in 1987 at the Santa Fe Indian Market. This honor was a first in the 66-year history of Indian Market for a rug or textile. Many top show awards—from Southwestern American Indian Arts Market, Navajo Nation Fair, Gallup Ceremonial and The Heard Museum—grace her walls. Today most of her rugs are woven for repeat buyers, plus the Indian Markets of the Heard Museum in Phoenix and Santa Fe. Rose Ann, Barbara's early mentor and soul-mate, was killed in an auto accident in 1996, along with her son and grandson. Soon after Rose Ann's death, a granddaughter was born into her family—the first girl in 20 years. Barbara now has a new goal: to teach her great-niece, Roxanne Rose, to weave, thus continuing the family circle of excellence.

Lorene Kee & Kathy White

There is a peaceful plateau southwest of Window Rock, Arizona, dense with pinon pines that hang heavy with nuts for the fall harvest. The summer sun is intense, but in the shade of a brush ramada, the gentle breeze is cooling. Lorene Kee weaves here during the summer with beauty all around her. In the distance, the soft tinkle of a ram's bell locates the flock. Lorene is a wisp of a lady, far too delicate to have endured a difficult life for 82 years. The eldest of four children, she and a sister, Mary Jane, are the only survivors.

When Lorene was 12, her mother died several months after giving birth to her sister. Her grandparents "hid her" from the Bureau of Indian Affairs (BIA) officials collecting children for boarding schools. She was needed to care for the younger children and to herd sheep. An aunt, Salt Water Woman, taught her to weave and she remembers her first rug, which was traded at the Pine Springs Trading Post. The whole family made the trip by wagon and enjoyed a picnic feast of store-bought bread and canned Vienna sausages with some of the trade money. Lorene was not yet a teen-ager, but she "felt great pride" in her accomplishment and the pleasure it brought her family.

When she was 19, Lorene found herself part of an "arranged marriage" that produced four children, but not a stable relationship. Years later and a single mother, she met Charley Kee while she was herding sheep. He met her "very secretly" for a year before they became man and wife. Six more children later, Lorene's family was complete. She never knew her sister, Mary Jane, who was raised by an Anglo nurse who befriended her dying mother. This only sister was educated at mission schools nearby and also received a nursing degree before moving to Los Angeles. The sisters were briefly united when Lorene was near death in 1967, but could not communicate because of the language difference. For two years, various medicines and "sings" failed to restore Lorene's health and the doctors "just gave up." It was a Christian pastor, whom she had heard over the radio, who came and prayed over her. Miraculously, "the next day she was well, healed by God," she believes. Eleven years ago, Rosita, Lorene's daughter, started a computer search and located Mary Ann again in California. Now the family has a reunion every year and, with the children as interpreters, the sisters can bridge the years.

Katherine Kee White, Lorene's 42-year-old daughter, has had a far different life. Lorene welcomed the chance for her children to "learn paper." Even though Kathy remembers crying when they were taken back to school in the fall, her parents knew the children would always be well fed and have good medical care. Summers were spent "playing store with old tin cans and green leaves for money." Everyone loaded into the horse-drawn wagon every week for the 10-mile round trip to the wells for water. Kathy's education included graduation from Many Farms High School and college in Prescott and Coolidge in Arizona. She was finishing a degree at Arizona State in Tempe when she met Fred White on a summer program with the Navajo Nation. After their marriage in 1987, both worked with tribal government for 10 years. Kathy is now a stay-at-home mom with their sons, Charleston and Jalen. Fred is Director of Tourism for the Navajo Nation. Kathy is weaving again and her motto is, "the more you do, the better you get." After 70 years at the loom, "Mom is a pro," Kathy adds with great pride.

Betty Nez

John Watchman was a firm believer in the "sheep is life" philosophy. His wife, Marie, was an excellent weaver and the mother of his 11 children. Betty Nez, 65, was the sixth child in this family. She attended day school in Sanders, Arizona, through the eighth grade. School came easily to her, but she was needed to tend the sheep and help in the home. There would be no more "learning paper". Now she can only wonder what type of job an education would have brought her. Two of her brothers went on to school in Oregon, but girls were expected to weave, herd and cook. She smiles now at her granddaughter, Mindy, when the five year old brings her paper and pencil and says, "Do your homework, Grandma."

Carding and spinning could be done while watching the sheep, but her mother's rugs were such a temptation. When Marie went to town, she always warned the children, "Don't touch my loom!" This is when Betty practiced her weaving, carefully removing her work before her mother's return. Her first rug was

completed when she was about 17, made from scraps of leftover wool. The $75 she earned made her feel "so happy and proud." Weaving has been her livelihood ever since. Large 5'x7' rugs can bring thousands of dollars, but the work is tedious and hard on the eyes and knees. Betty's new hogan was recently built by her family, but is not hooked to electricity. She still weaves with a kerosene lamp on each side of the loom. She remembers many times working at her loom until midnight and starting again at 4 a.m. to finish a rug.

In addition to Mindy, there are 25 other grandchildren and seven great-grands. Betty enjoys having several of her children living on her home site. She is "happiest" when she is busy. Her daughter, Beverly, insists that "mom always puts herself last. If she is not helping her kids, she helps her siblings." Right now a brother needs to be picked up at a Flagstaff hospital and Betty is ready for the 300 mile round-trip. Families come first with the Navajo.

Beverly Nez

Living on the same "home site" as her mother, Betty Nez (pg 39), Beverly Nez represents the 30-something generation. Her house is a large mobile home with electricity to power television and computers. Her cell phone is her link to beyond the reservation. She is a single mom of five children, ranging in age from five to 14. A graduate of Sanders High School, Beverly currently works for the Burlington Northern/Santa Fe Railroad. She is a security guard for railroad equipment wherever work is being done, from Lupton, Arizona, to Barstow, California. Grandma Betty, and her sister, Tammy, are available as child-sitters. Beverly has the strong determination needed to make this work. Her sunny disposition and great sense of humor serve her well.

Beverly grew up as somewhat of a tomboy, riding horses and playing with her brothers. She likes to build things and played a large part in the construction of her mother's new hogan. Lack of financing made her postpone further education, but she still wants a college degree. The nursing field is one interest and pipe-fitting another. Her brother, Mark, is a welder and she would love to work tandem with him. This would be a chance to greatly increase her earning power for her education and that of her children. Meanwhile, weaving is a constant source of extra income. She started when her first child was born and she was homebound. The round rug she has "up" is semi-circles of different patterns, using the same color tones. It is portable, so she can take it on the road with her.

"Keep yourself happy and your children will be happy," she believes. She also believes in exercise—lifting weights and jogging to stay in shape. She always tries to talk out problems with her kids. "Education is the key" and she urges them to keep their grades up to qualify for scholarships. Her parents were always supportive of her and she will be the same. "Don't give up, always keep going and take every step ahead possible" is her motto. With that winning smile, Beverly adds, "My kids are my wealth!"

Mae Clark

Mae Clark, her husband Jackson, son Nocona, and daughter Shyn, live just south of Burnham Trading Post in Sanders, Arizona. This area is called New Lands. The family was relocated from the Rocky Ridge-Big Mountain area of Arizona in 1996 because of the ongoing Hopi/Navajo land dispute. Mae's birthplace is located 100 miles north of Winslow, Arizona, where her mother still lives. Fourth generation trader Bruce Burnham remembers first seeing Mae as a cute toddler in the back of her mother's wagon outside the old Dennebito Trading Post. Her family had 100 head of sheep, many of the them the cherished Churro breed Mae and her brother grew up herding. She first attended Rocky Ridge Boarding School, followed by Tuba City with graduation from Many Farms High School. Education was very important to her father, Tohannie Begay, so Mae went on to Northern Arizona University in Flagstaff, Arizona. When her father became ill, she left the university to help care for him.

Her first rug, at 20, was a Storm Pattern. She sold it to Elijah Blair, the trader at Dennebito, for $50. The money was used to buy powdered milk for her lambs along with some hay. Mae's father was a strong influence on her early life. He urged her to strive for perfection in her weaving—"no mistakes, make it perfect." At the same time, he cautioned her to never look at a rug in progress and think "damn, I'm good!" Before his untimely death in 1994, Tohannie told his daughter "never mistreat a rug" because "it has a soul and a spirit." Tears come to Mae's eyes as she remembers him.

After the move to New Lands, Mae reconnected with Bruce at the Burnham Trading Post. She used his bright palette of yarns to weave

Germantown rugs reminiscent of the "Long Walk" period. Depressed over the loss of her dad, Mae was able keep harmony in her life with time at her loom. She added landscapes to her weaving patterns and a rug she calls, "Four Generations." The first figure depicts a great-grandmother in the traditional garb of post Bosque Redondo (1868-1880), holding a second phase Chief Blanket. The grandmother wears the tiered skirt with a crushed velvet blouse and carries a Germantown weaving (1868-1905). The mother figure is dressed in a woven Navajo Beal dress with a sash belt, moccasins and buckskin leg wraps. Her rug is a Ganado Red, popular in the mid 1900s. The daughter wears high platform heels, a mini-skirt and three earrings. She holds a modern Germantown Renaissance Rug, a current trend of artists who feel empowered to innovate and experiment. These rugs are fun to make and Mae can easily meet her daily goal of many inches. She can spend eight to 10 hours per day weaving, especially when her children are in school. School for the kids is currently at Wide Ruins, Arizona. This is Mae and Jackson's choice because of a strong program in traditional values and the teaching of Navajo as a second language.

To keep balance in her life, Mae has a "Blessing Way" ceremony with the medicine man every four years. She never forces herself to weave or does it when she feels anger. She grew up hearing the "tapping sound of the comb on weft" and to this day it makes her feel "most secure." Her late father told her to make a name for herself, and thanks to the encouragement of Bruce Burnham and her family, she feels she's "almost there!"

Elouise Lee

The "rug room" at the Burnham Trading Post in Sanders, Arizona, is alive with the laughter of the Lee family. Mom, Elouise, and her four daughters are typical of many modern Navajo families—busy with jobs and school, but adhering to traditional ways and speaking both English and Navajo. Elouise's daughters are Cherish, 16, Chyrell, 13, Chancee, 10, and Dannee, 7. Her sons are Herchel and Wendell King, who is married with two children of his own. The Lee compound also includes the homes of grandparents, aunts, uncles and cousins. Father, Danny Lee, works for the government in the Chambers Range Office. Members of this close extended family all contribute to the girls' educations. Just as Elouise learned to weave from her grandmothers, they are taught to make tamales, butcher, tend livestock, help their medicine man Grandpa and assist as auto mechanics—all from family members within walking distance. From their happy smiles, you know life is fun!

Elouise has worked at the Trading Post for eight years and the Burnhams consider her "a most dependable employee." When her daughters are off to school, she heads for a full day of work and still has time to weave Eye Dazzler and Germantown rugs during evenings and days off. Her daughters are all weaving, even Dannee, who started at age four. Their dad helps with color selections and pattern suggestions. Family celebrations are usually at the Lee house, but Sunday dinners find everyone at Grandma's. Because both parents work, the girls have many chores after school—making dinner, hauling wood and feeding the animals. A new addition is a llama named Cisco, who acts as the sheep herder.

The girls also create "dreamcatchers," which according to Navajo legend, capture bad dreams when hung over the bed. Their schools include "culture classes," to instill the traditional ways and values also taught at home. Everyone speaks two languages and will learn another in high school. The children can speak their native tongue to their grandparents, so important to learn stories of the old ways. In answer to future plans, "inventor, lawyer, astronaut and basketball player" seem to be the favorites. The Lee family loves trips to visit relatives in Colorado and a forest ranger uncle in Rocky Mountain National Park.

The Navajo culture is matriarchal and Elouise fills her role well. The only complaints about Mom are that "she is too serious" and "moves too fast when teaching weaving." Check the smiles and feel the respect—Mom is very special in this home. These lovely ladies will be well trained for life, but Dad says, "No marriage until they are at least 30!"

Rose Yazzie

This is a special day for 62-year-old Rose Yazzie. Her extended family, or "outfit", is making the trip to their old summer hogan in the depths of Canyon de Chelly. The mouth of the canyon is located just east of Chinle, Arizona, a place which means "water flowing." The first residents of the canyon were probably the Anasazi from approximately 500 to 1300 A.D. The ruins of their pueblo-style dwellings still cling under the rock ledges in the towering canyon walls. Pictographs leave a chiseled history of these "Ancient Ones." The canyon is sacred to the Navajo who made this their home in the 17th century. The fertile bottom land with a plentiful water supply, grew their corn and melons and provided grazing for the livestock. Spider Woman, according to Navajo legend, lived atop Spider Rock and taught The People to weave. Rose's hogan sits at the base of this majestic red pillar.

Pickup loads of the Tabaaha clan, led by the matriarch Rose, drive the broad sand highway into the canyon. Tourists must take special vehicles or drive themselves accompanied by a Navajo guide. Hiking down 1 1/4 miles from White House Overlook on the south rim is the only other option. The canyon walls grow taller with each turn and the colors become more breathtaking. Rose's four daughters spent summers here, herding the sheep, catching minnows in the cool water and learning to weave at her side. From the few remaining peach trees, the girls dried fruit on rocks in the sun. They remember a rope swing in a large cottonwood tree, bread dipped in goat's milk for breakfast and long happy days filled with family laughter.

A few years ago, Rose decided to take some of her 18 grandchildren down for a summer hogan experience. Each day she woke them before sun-up to gather wood and carry water. Their attempts with a cake mix turned into a real disaster in the wood-fired oven. There was no television or fast food. They had to make fires at night to scare the coyotes away from the sheep corrals. The loud chorus of complaints ended with "no cold pop!" The family compound on the south canyon rim looked wonderful to the kids upon their return.

Rose's four daughters and six grandchildren all are recognized weavers. When granddaughters, Harriet and LaVera, were in their early teens, they created a "Spider Rock Design," that has become a family favorite. It is a black stepped pattern on a background using the bright palette of colors available in commercial wool. Rose sold her first rug at the old Garcia's Trading Post for one dollar. Now these gifted weavers get prices in the thousands of dollars.

In late 1863, Kit Carson and his troops marched on Canyon de Chelly, pillaging and burning the Navajos' crops and killing their precious "Churro" sheep herds. The peach orchards were destroyed. Women and children were kidnapped and forced into slavery. Starving and freezing with cold, more than 3,000 souls surrendered and were forced to march more than 300 miles to Bosque Redondo near Fort Sumner, New Mexico. "The Long Walk" was "hwelte," meaning a time of dread and fear, and the beginning of four miserable years of incarceration. These canyon walls have witnessed much sadness, but today, they are once again sacred homeland to the Navajo.

Rose Singer Maloney & Laura

The soft lines of a face can be a road map of life's travails, but eyes that sparkle and the hint of a smile tell of the soul and spirit within. Rose Singer Maloney has such a face. She was born near Gray Mountain, Arizona, and has spent her 83 years in the harsh landscape of the western reservation. Slim and Fannie Singer had eight children and only Rose and a sister remain. The family had livestock—sheep, cattle and horses, and a constant battle with Mormon settlers and other Anglos for grazing lands. In 1918, President Wilson gave the Navajos 94,000 acres in this area through an executive order, but disputes took years to settle.

Rose was close to her father and liked herding the animals, but as the oldest daughter she also was in charge of her younger siblings. Several times she attempted to run away. If she had been allowed to attend school, she "would not be on the reservation now." She feared her mother, but her weaving skills came from her. Fannie also warned her that weaving tools "were sacred" and always should be kept in their special bag. When she was nine, Rose sold a saddle blanket, her first project, for $4 in trade. Storm Pattern designs always have been her

favorite. Her sheep supplied the wool until a move to Cameron, Arizona, in 1975, when the flock was sold.

Rose raised a family of eight children. Daughter, Laura Ann Singer, was seriously ill as a little girl and spent much of her childhood away from home in hospitals and boarding schools. Now Laura and Rose enjoy living together. Both are fine weavers and help-mates to each other. Together they make the trip to Hubbell Trading Post at Ganado, Arizona, more than 140 miles away, to sell their rugs.

The Storm Pattern designs of the western reservation date back to the early 1900s. The borders feature stylized zigzags and steps, with corners of squares and rectangles framing an elaborate center box of intricate geometric designs. Traditionally the colors were red, black and white on a gray background. They can also contain complex Navajo symbolism.

This arid land of fossilized dinosaurs and petrified remains resembles a moonscape. In 1971, astronauts practiced driving a lunar craft on this rocky terrain. The Navajo weaver sees beauty in this stark landscape, in violent storms and lightning, transforming them into rugs that will grace any wall.

Marjorie Spencer

If you ever need a traveling companion, just call Marjorie Spencer. She can pack in a minute and loves to see places beyond the reservation. This lovely 66-year-old lady is the mother of four daughters who like to take Mom on trips with them. Daughter, Brenda (pg. 11), has included her on trips to Hong Kong and New York City. Recently her grandson, Deverell, graduated from St. Johns High School in Arizona and wanted to go to Spokane, Washington, to visit his aunt and cousins. He was told he could not go alone, so he chose to go with Grandma. Marjorie was flattered to accompany the 18-year-old boy.

Marjorie is the daughter of Buine Roanhorse and Mamie Burnside. Her only sibling was a brother, Francis, who was four years older. They lived near Chambers, Arizona, at a place called Indian Village. Both parents worked as silversmiths there. Life was full of a steady stream of tourists with news from beyond the reservation. After school at nearby Sanders, Marjorie was ready to further expand her world by attending the Indian Boarding School in Albuquerque, New Mexico. It was there that she was first exposed to weaving and other arts and crafts.

After her marriage and the birth of her first child, an aunt, Fannie Lee, let her help with a Wide Ruins rug she was weaving. Fannie sold the rug and Marjorie became aware that there was money to be made at the loom. She got a late start at 28-years-old, but has been weaving ever since. She has won competitions in Gallup, New Mexico as well as in Flagstaff and Casa Grande, Arizona. Had she finished school, her early dreams were of being a teacher. Instead she has taught her daughters to be excellent weavers. Brenda and Geneva Scott Shabi (pg 17) share her home site at Wide Ruins, Arizona, along with other family members.

This family of weavers has a special signature to identify their rugs. They weave a 1/2-inch stripe using all the colors at each end of the rug. Check the "rug room" at Hubbell Trading Post in Ganado, Arizona, for their work.

Mary Foghorn

Shiprock, New Mexico, is named after an impressive rock formation that resembles a boat under full sail. Located just southwest of the town, the formation juts more than 7,000 feet into the azure sky and is a landmark to a population of 8,000—a large town by reservation standards. The Shiprock Trading Post also is a historic location and owner Jed Foutz represents generations of Foutz traders, a name well known to the area. Mary Foghorn sells her rugs here and also gets to visit with her son, Curtis, who is a valued post employee. Mary and her husband, John, have been married for 45 years and have seven children and 20 grandchildren. They are beginning to feel the years, but their children insist they "are not old!"

Mary was born to Marie Blacksheep and Little Joe, the second of five children. She spent six years at the Toadlena Boarding School, always missing her family and longing for Christmas vacation and summers. She loved to herd sheep and goats with her brother and learned to card and spin on the high desert mesas. Before the intense heat of the summer, the herd was taken up into the Chuska Mountains in search of greener pastures and cool breezes. The trip took two days with an overnight at Toadlena. Her mother would weave under the cedar trees at their "sheep camp." These were family times, safe and secure in their land of endless horizons.

John Foghorn is a United States Army veteran of the Korean War. Curtis only has heard him speak of his war experiences once. One Christmas he told his family the things he had to do "were not very nice," a direct conflict with the Navajo's life of harmony with nature. Both parents are proud of their youngest son, John Jr., a firefighter who was having a busy season during the summer of 2002. John Sr. is retired from railroad work and today both he and Mary tend 107 head of sheep and goats. Mary's fine Two Grey Hills rugs are made of the delicate earth tones of their fleece.

John and Mary Foghorn are very traditional Navajos. Family and sheep are the center of their lives. Their son, Curtis, proudly calls them "the very best parents, always patient." He recalls playing in his grandmother's old hogan on one occasion that could have been a disaster. The game was "Horse" and brother David was "it." He tucked a string tail into the back of his pants. To add to the excitement, he had dipped the "tail" in kerosene and someone in the group lit it.

David became a bucking horse and still bears a scar on his back as a reminder of this childhood mischief. Mary worries about her grandchildren now. The youngest one, Max, is 18 months old and always greets grandma "with a great big hug!" This sweet lady "walks in beauty." She brings harmony to the many lives she touches and a special magic to her loom.

54

Brenda Crosby

Brenda Crosby was born in a hogan near Many Farms, Arizona. She was the seventh of 13 children. Due to family circumstances, she was raised as an only child by her grandmother, Mary Billy, and an aunt, Grace Grey. There were cousins nearby for playmates and her life was a happy one. She attended elementary school in Many Farms, middle school in Kayenta and high school at Chinle and Many Farms Boarding Schools. When Brenda was in her late teens, her grandmother told her about her other siblings. She left school before graduation to raise the four youngest in a "mutual house" at Many Farms. Navajos paid rent to the United States government for these dwellings and eventually owned them. They were located close to schools so children had easy access to public education. This home remains in Brenda's family.

When she was 14, Brenda wove her first striped rug with Mary Billy's help and hand-prepared wool. She next attempted Yei (Holy People) patterns and large Pictorials. All went well until Brenda was in her early 20s and began to suffer from serious depression, panic and anxiety attacks. Kee Charlie Yazzie, a relative and medicine man, did a Blessing Way for her in an attempt to bring balance to her young life. She sat on the sandpaintings he created for her while he sang the curing songs. Harmony and order finally were restored to her life and Kee assured her that she could safely make Sandpainting rugs. These rugs are now her specialty—Night Skies, Feather People, Father Sky and Mother Earth. They teach the Navajo legends of creation in delicate earth tones. Brenda feels she has a God-given talent as a result of this difficult period in her life. People who purchase her rugs believe they bring good luck and instill a calming atmosphere to their homes. Brenda continues to have the Blessing ceremony done for her every four years.

Brenda's four children, two sons and two daughters, reflect her love of reading and value of education. Tara will soon graduate from San Juan College in Farmington, New Mexico, and hopes to continue her studies of architecture in Europe. She speaks four languages. Daughter, Judy, has chosen a career in the United States Army. The family hopes to visit her next summer while she is on a tour of duty in Hawaii. The boys, Darrick and Clint, do not speak or understand the Navajo language as well as the girls, so they have been part of bilingual classes in school. Brenda wants all of her children to know Navajo history and to be proud of their noble heritage.

In 2000, Brenda along with Tara, Darrick, and her sister, Bertha, accompanied Shiprock trader, Jed Foutz, to Washington D.C., as guests of the United States Department of the Interior. Brenda and Bertha demonstrated weaving in the Craft Shop there for a week. The family got a first-hand view of the United States government and saw many historical sights. This was the first flight for Brenda and her family. Leaving the Albuquerque, New Mexico, airport, they clung tightly to each other as the pilot pointed out the sights below to these true Native Americans.

Florence Riggs

Beryl, Utah, was the birthplace of 39-year-old Florence Riggs. Her family was involved in the potato harvest there. The family's home was in Sand Springs, Arizona, located on southeastern Hopi land. This area became part of the Relocation Program. In 1978, Louise Y. and Hosteen Nez moved their family of eight children first to Flagstaff and finally to Tuba City. The Nez family owned livestock—sheep, cattle and horses. The children attended boarding school in Leupp, Arizona, and Tuba City Boarding High School. Summers were special times spent with family and herding sheep on horseback. The nearest water hole and trees for shade were five miles away. Sheep and herders made the round trip each day. Mother, Louise, made clay toys for her children to play with, the forerunners of the now popular Navajo folk art. This family also played the "Horse" game of tag and rolled old tires to simulate driving cars.

Like many Navajo women, Florence's grandmother, Laura A. Nez, inspired and encouraged her weaving. Florence completed her first small Two Grey Hills rug when she was 18 and sold it to her brother, Leo, for $50. She wove Sandpainting rugs until she experienced some "spiritual encounters," causing pain in her arms and back when she sat at the loom. She credits her Christian family background with helping her overcome the pain. She no longer makes Sandpainting rugs, but specializes in Pictorials, rug dresses and traditional designs. Her imagination can run the gamut of expression—reservation landscapes, trading post interiors or any scenes she sees in her travels. Florence is pictured in a dress she created for her only daughter Marietta's graduation from high school.

Marietta and her brother, Adrian attend Pima Community College in Tucson, Arizona. Marietta is on the cross-country team and is busy with college life. When she shows interest, Florence will be glad to "put a rug up" for her. Weaving has taken Florence to Santa Fe, New Mexico, to participate in the Weavers Image Show and to the Albuquerque Museum to demonstrate weaving techniques.

She feels her weavings help "explain her culture." Since an Indian art publication showed one of Florence's rugs with another weaver's name, she signs her rugs with her initials in the lower left corner. Be sure to look if you want a Florence Riggs original.

Dennis Long

Dennis Long is unique in several ways. He is a 42-year-old male weaver who lives in the silent world of the deaf. He was born in Shiprock, New Mexico, to the late Mary and Jack Long. His mother was devoted to protecting her only child, after losing four babies in pregnancy. Grandparents and clan members wove a safe cocoon around young Dennis to insulate him from the outside world. His home has always been in Teec Nos Pos, which means "Trees in a Circle." Always at his mother's side, the young boy learned beadwork, cooking, sewing and pottery. His first venture into the outside world was to New Mexico's School for the Deaf in Santa Fe. There, he learned to sign in both Navajo and English. Dennis is tall and fit, so he played both basketball and soccer.

Mary Long was an excellent weaver and saw Navajo rugs as a means of income for her son. The two of them completed a rug when Dennis was 20. They sold it at Shiprock Trading Post for $500. Imagine Mary's relief to know that her son would be able to support himself. After Mary's recent death, Dennis lives with his adopted sister, Marie. His Yei and Yeibichais rugs are typical of the Shiprock area. Yeis (deities) face forward, usually with three to six figures surrounded by the elongated body of

the "rainbow goddess." Yeibichais are depicted as dancers in profile and can be male or female. Dennis also does elaborate Sandpainting rugs. He feels that in some cases "being both deaf and male makes him special to his buyers."

Dennis's life is a mobile one, thanks to his pick-up truck. When in public places, he often has a difficult time communicating since he does not speak at all. He can easily be misunderstood for not answering a question or offering an apology. Dennis is a bachelor and likes his independence. "No lady to ask when (he) will be home or where (he) is going!" He dresses very neatly and is proud when the girls say he "always smells nice." He looks quite handsome wearing an 1860s Churro wool and bayeta serape in a doorway at the Shiprock Trading Post.

Dennis is proud to be a Navajo and a weaver. "It takes a lot of patience to complete a rug. My mind is always on the wefts and keeping track of the warps," he writes. He is happy to know that readers might be interested in his life. With both parents gone, he must live with only their memories. He is grateful for Marie's care. He wants the reader to know that "my mom is always part of each of my weavings."

Mary Ann Foster

In the historic old Toadlena (New Mexico) Trading Post/Museum hangs a wonderful textile show titled "Dances with Wool." Trader Mark Winter has used his artistic genius to display the finest of Sandpainting designs. One of the featured weavers is Mary Ann Foster. Mother Earth and Father Sky dominate the various symbols used in curing ceremonies that appear in these rugs. She first attempted a Yeibichai design, when called on to help her cousin, Patsy, finish a project. Mary is a Christian and does not feel that duplicating the designs made by medicine men is harmful. She hopes that her rugs will bring good luck as well as pleasure to her many buyers. Mary Ann is content to stay on her high desert plateau near the Chuska Mountains and create masterpieces.

Born to Jane and Jim Foster at Sheep Springs, New Mexico, Mary Ann was one of 16 children. To this family, "weaving was a way of life". The girls "played at" learning to herd, card, spin and, finally, make a rug of their own. On a two-sided loom, Mary Ann and her sister, Susan, started together. When she was 10, Mary Ann rode her horse to the Two Grey Hills Trading Post to sell her first woven saddle blanket. The ten dollars she received was a fortune to her and she realized that weaving could provide much needed income.

At 75, Mary Ann is still a beautiful woman. As a young maiden at the local squaw dances, she easily stole the heart of a young man named Harry. They were married when she was only 15. Harry worked for the Union Pacific Railroad until his retirement some years ago. Two sons were born to the couple and the youngest, Phillip, still lives with them. Their oldest son, Clement, died of complications from pneumonia and chicken pox at the age of 7, when he was away at boarding school. As a result, Phillip was sent to day school at Newcomb and describes his mother as "overprotective".

There still is a "sheep camp" in the Chuska Mountains where the summer air is cooler and the grass is more plentiful. The Fosters no longer make the trip up in a wagon with a team, but life does follow many of the old patterns. The tiny Christian Reformed Church where they were married remains down the road from the trading post and little Clement's grave is in the small cemetery there. Mark Winter calls Mary Ann "the master of sandpainting rugs." With the help of her son and husband, she continues to weave her special magic.

Delana Farley

Navajo young people preparing for careers and adulthood must straddle the line between reservation life and the world beyond. Delana Farley is spending the summer following her graduation from Newcomb High School, working away from home in Farmington, New Mexico. With youthful exuberance, she looks ahead to attending the Institute of American Indian Arts in Santa Fe in the fall of 2002. She is an outstanding student—taking Advanced Placement courses and involved in sports and student government. The bumper sticker on her car says "National Honor Society" and she served as the president. Delana also led the student council and her junior class. She was part of the first weaving class of four students at Newcomb High School—now the course has over 30 enrolled. Living in Santa Fe will take her away from her close family—mom Sarah, dad Gilbert, sister Pamela, brother Roland and a tiny nephew, Devin. The Farley home and hogan sit on a high wind-swept desert plateau guarded by Beautiful Mountain, Bennett Peak, and Ford Butte. The peak is named after F. T. Bennett, a US Army Captain with genuine concern for the Navajo in the troubled years after the Long Walk. He was affectionately called "Big Belly" by The People.

Delana's mother, Sarah Farley, learned to weave from her mother, Helen Manygoats, who is now in her early 80s. Her home is just over a ridge, protected by a small grove of trees. Married couples remain close to the wife's family in this matriarchal society. Extended family includes many cousins, aunts and uncles.

Grandpa Manygoats is a medicine man, though no longer able to do many "sings." The entire family just participated in a ceremony, "The Beauty Way," given for one of Sarah's brothers returning from a long stay in Oklahoma. There were two nights of prayers and cleansing to restore harmony in his life and prepare him for new things. These Navajo traditions will continue to be part of young Delana's life as she studies in Santa Fe. Weaving will always be a link between the three generations.

Gilbert Farley suffered a serious spinal injury as a young man and spent much time in hospitals. Luckily, Sarah Manygoats worked in one of them. He had to wear leg braces and use a wheelchair, but his outgoing sense of humor won her heart. With amazing determination, he now walks unassisted and built the hogan on their home site by himself. He tends the sheep and does beadwork while Sarah works as a teacher's aid in a Shiprock elementary school. Gilbert loves to joke—he even convinced a very young Delana that she was half-Ute, a tribe not always in harmony with the Navajos. Much to his dismay, she told her teachers at school. She is not so gullible now. She knows who she is and has ideas of what she wants to do with her life—perhaps social work or something in the medical field since she "loves to help elderly people and children." Art will always play a part in her life. As she told the San Juan Sun newspaper when she was a freshman, "I want to make lots of money." Delana is ready and able to handle both worlds.

Eleanor Lameman & Carmelita Sagg

All Navajo people seem to have a delightful sense of humor. Carmelita Sagg and her mother, Eleanor Lameman, laugh and giggle as they talk of family life in their "compound" east of Mexican Water, Arizona. Eleanor is 67, the daughter of Edith and Cowboy Lameman, born in a summer "shade house" near Aneth, Utah. She was the only girl of four children, so was not allowed to go to school. She was needed to herd sheep, cattle and horses and help with the cooking. She rode a donkey named "Fluffy" while herding and he occasionally bucked her off. She remembers that landing in the Rabbit Brush was very painful and some falls were hard enough to knock her briefly unconscious. Her paternal grandmother (Nali), known to everyone as Mr. Blackwater's Daughter, taught her to weave when she was nine. By age 12, the trade money for rugs bought shoes and material to make clothes.

Eleanor has four children. Carmelita is her only daughter and the oldest. Eleanor's children went to Teec Nos Pos Boarding School with the luxuries of electricity and running water. Carmelita loved reading, math and English, and was able to cover all her school expenses at Red Mesa High School weaving like her mother. She also spent summers herding, but read books while atop her Palomino horse. One day, something spooked her mount and she went sailing along with her book. It was a long walk home to face her brothers' teasing.

Weaving is the only source of income for Eleanor, but Carmelita has always had a full-time job. She has been a technical assistant for federal programs, a teaching assistant and is currently the secretary for the Transportation/Maintenance Department of the Red Mesa School District. She also holds the elected office of Secretary/Treasurer for the Mexican Water Chapter House of the Navajo Nation.

Both mother and daughter can weave the traditional styles of Two Grey Hills, Teec Nos Pos and Ganado Reds. Trader Steve Simpson encourages them to weave "specialty designs" with more contemporary patterns of mosaics and crosses. Some of these are from artists renderings. Eleanor always dreamed of being a singer and likes to sing traditional and "church songs" at her loom. She warns never to eat while weaving.

When the family gathers for holidays, the children all help with the cooking. On Sundays, Grandma usually has some mutton stew and frybread ready for anyone who drops in. Carmelita plays the "favorite auntie" role and admits to spoiling her seven nieces and nephews. Nephew Ryan loves to go to Farmington with her for toys and "Chinese food." His only criticism of auntie is that, "she talks an awful lot!"

Veronica Six

At 36, Veronica Six is as harried as any young mother of five children. Her youngest, Marla, is in third grade, allowing her time to explore the job market. Currently she is part of a training program for employment in the Food Service Department at Pine Spring Community School. Veronica, the second of eight children, was raised in Gallup, New Mexico by her mother, Minnie James. She attended various boarding schools and was first exposed to weaving at Fort Wingate High School. Athletics—volleyball in particular—were favorite activities in her teen years. Her biological family did not weave.

Living at the eastern fringe of the reservation, Veronica learned most about Navajo tradition from her mother-in-law, Bah Yazzie Ashley (pg 3). When she was 22, Bah put a rug up for her and "told her to weave." The rug she had made in school was a simple design of squares and steps, which she sold at Burnham Trading Post for $100. From that school experience, exposure to Bah and a genetic tendency to design, Veronica produced a Wide Ruins style rug. She has woven ever since. As she is working on a rug, she also is planning ahead for the next one. Germantown rugs, with their bright spectrum of colors, really suit her style. Veronica is full of energy and smiles.

Her wedding was a traditional Navajo ceremony. Assisted by the Ashley family, she ground the corn to make the mush which is eaten by the couple from the wedding basket. She made her wedding gown from peach-colored satin and velvet. Preparations consume the entire wedding day with much cooking as people arrive from various parts of the reservation. The medicine man performed the ceremony outside under a brush ramada. Veronica's first child was born when she was 21.

John Ashley, Veronica's father-in-law, was another great influence on her life. He was her father figure, "always there for her", and treating her with "much respect." Later in his life, he suffered from diabetes and was hard of hearing. Veronica was able to convince him to go the doctor and tolerate dialysis. He was a difficult patient, not happy with the diet or the necessary care. Diabetes is common among the Navajo. John died from complications of the disease and fighting "the white man's medicine." Fortunately today, clinics all over the reservation help "The People" deal with this illness.

Jalayne Gould

On a balmy Saturday in September, Jalayne Gould has come to the revered Toadlena Trading Post in New Mexico, with her father and sister. The weathered sandstone building dates back to 1909 and bustles with activity on this special day. Trader Mark Winter and his wife, Lerin, purchased the post in 1997 and are hosting a "Carding and Spinning Celebration" for local weavers and many of their families. The patio behind the Post is a tapestry of color with groups of ladies of all ages and in every hue of cotton and velvet. They wear their finest Navajo silver and turquoise jewelry which gleams in the autumn sun. This is a time for camaraderie, exchange of ideas, story-telling and a hearty lunch. Phyllis and Chuck Kinsey, the managers of Toadlena Trading Post, and their staff have planned for days preparing a feast of mutton stew, fry bread, roasted lamb and sweets for dessert. The conversations are soft and mostly in the fluid beauty of the Navajo language. Jalayne, at 16, must be both in awe and inspired by all the activity.

She has been involved in weaving classes under art instructor, Barbara Thomas, as part of the curriculum at Newcomb High School.

Jalayne is a senior, and will be a 2003 graduate. Toadlena and the Winters have been the original sponsors of this popular program. Local weavers have donated both their time and expertise along with fleece from their flocks. The young weavers are encouraged to enter competitions in New Mexico and Arizona. Jalayne proudly displays her second place rug from the Wheelwright Museum Invitational for Young Native American Artists, held in June 2001 in Santa Fe. The cash prize is welcome to any teen-ager, but she glows with pride before these weaving masters.

Jalayne first helped her mother, Darlene, weave when she was only seven years old. She finds that working at her loom has a calming effect. The tensions of school and adolescence fade away. She gets lost in the patterns of her thoughts and the rug that is taking shape. She is still learning the carding and spinning process. During the summer school break, she can easily spend half a day at the loom. She improves with each rug. The Toadlena/Two Grey Hills legacy of weaving excellence must seem daunting to one so young. When will her work be "Best of Show" in Santa Fe or the Ceremonial in Gallup?

Jennie Slick

Jennie Slick is pictured in the "Rug Room" of the Burnham Trading Post at Sanders, Arizona, surrounded by an outstanding collection of Germantown rugs. These are the by-products of the four-year incarceration at Bosque Redondo, following the "Long Walk." The Navajo people had watched their hogans, peach orchards and sheep herds be destroyed by Kit Carson's troops. Those surviving the 300-mile march in 1864 found themselves at Fort Sumner, New Mexico, with nothing to occupy their time. The United States government furnished them with some clothing, and brightly colored blankets made at Germantown, Pennsylvania, mills. The weavers were able to unravel the cloth and make garments of their liking. The designs took on a serape look and were decorated with fringe. The Indian Agents finally took note and had skeins of yarn shipped to the Navajos, so that they might continue weaving. Today, the Germantown Navajo Rug is a beautiful testament to this dark period of history for "The People."

Jennie is 54 years old and she knows the history of the Navajo. As the fourth child of nine and the oldest daughter of Anna and John Ashley, she would have been a nurse if she had not dropped out of school in her teens. Married life in California and five children followed by a divorce, brought Jennie home to Arizona and the loom at age 39. Her first rug had been sold to Ortegas' Trading Post when she was 16. Now weaving would become a means of support for her family. "It gives you a good feeling to have a rug up," she smiles. She first checks her available wool, selects colors and then lets the spirit of the rug take over—the artist's touch speaks through the design. When asked to do a certain pattern or colors for a buyer, she often "struggles." Burnt Water and Germantowns are her favorites, using the palette of colors available at Burnhams'. Jennie once created a 9'x12' masterpiece that took a year to complete. During this time, she also completed smaller rugs to supplement her income.

Today, Jennie balances her weaving with a full-time job as an elderly homecare provider. The old dream of nursing is finding fulfillment. She is so proud of her youngest sibling, Anna, who graduated as a dental assistant with her family applauding her achievement. Jennie also teaches weaving to Anglos several times a year. She takes great pride in representing Navajo artists. After her students experience the amount of time and skill necessary to produce a rug, the market price makes much more sense. Several of her grandchildren are involved in school weaving programs, so the tradition lives on.

Bill Malone

TRADER

I was born in Gallup, New Mexico in 1939. In the early 1950s our family moved to Texas and then to Colorado. After getting out of the army in February 1961, I came back to Gallup and later started working for Al Frick at Lupton Trading Post in Lupton, Arizona. It was there I got the itch to get into the trading business.

I also met a Navajo girl, Minnie Goodluck, who became my wife. Our family grew to one boy and four girls at Pinon. We soon moved to Keams Canyon, Arizona to work at the Pinon Mercantile for the McGee family. I worked at the Trading Post and my wife became postmaster for Pinon. She was also a great silversmith and weaver.

It was at Pinon where I learned about Navajo rugs from my employer, Cliff McGee. Pinon was the home of big Navajo rugs. It was not uncommon to have 20 or 30 big rugs rolled up in the basement rug room. It was there I met traders J.B. Tanner, Joe Tanner, John Kennedy and Tobe Turpen Jr. I feel I had an impact on other traders including Bruce McGee, Al Grieve, Bruce Burnham and Steve Getzwiller.

In May of 1981, I was selected to become Trader/Manager at Hubbell Trading Post in Ganado, Arizona. It was sad to leave as we had made many wonderful friends in Pinon. One nice thing for our kids was that the Ganado school was only a mile away,

unlike Pinon, where it was 48 miles away.

Coming to Hubbell was a big change as there was more interaction in the rug business. Hubbell has always been known for its red rugs. Ganado is the hub for weavers from Chinle, Pinon, Klagetoh and Wide Ruins. It is the crossroads for the buyer and the seller.

Since I have been here most of the local trading posts have gone out of business. This has made Hubbell the place to find rugs from other Trading Posts that are not in business like Klagetoh, Wide Ruins, Burntwater, Crystal and others.

It is not uncommon to buy a rug from a grandmother and a granddaughter on the same day. Grandmothers 80 to 90 years old still bring in their rugs and girls as young as 6 years old also. It a great place to come and see that interaction between the weaver and the trader. Many times weavers will travel three hours or more to bring in their rugs.

I have been at Hubbell for the past 21 years and it seems like the time has just flown by. I am truly glad that Hubbell Trading Post became a National Park Service Historic Site in 1967, so weavers and buyers can enjoy it now and into the future. What more can I say, except come by and see Hubbell Trading Post.

Hubbell Trading Post—Ganado, Arizona

Jed Foutz

TRADER

Throughout history weaving has been a central and intrinsic element of Navajo Culture. As part of the Navajo Creation Story, weaving is viewed as a gift from Spiderwoman. Many of the earliest historical references to the Navajo refer to weavers and the unsurpassed beauty and technical aptitude of their blankets. Weaving is a way of life: to be Navajo is to weave: to weave is to be Navajo. These truths are inseparably interwoven to form one of the core foundations of Navajo culture.

As a boy, I often had the opportunity to travel with my father on "rug" trips calling on shops and galleries across the western United States. As my father was selling, he would educate the staff or gallery owner by recounting details and stories about individual weavers and their weavings. Invariably the question "how do you determine a great Navajo rug" would be asked. The stage was set. Letting the question hang, Dad would show a few more weavings. Then he would reach over to the "great" stack, always shown last, and unfold the "best" rug in his inventory. The response was always immediate—oohs and ahs—"That is how you know a great weaving."

If regarded only on the basis of technical and artistic merit, Navajo weavings are masterpieces. Evenly woven, complex unscripted patterns of extraordinary palette, framed by straight selvage. However, this is only a glimpse of a weaving. It is the experiences, beliefs, songs, stories, prayers and ceremonies woven between the weft and the warp that lie at the heart of their beauty and value. The weaving is a projection of the weaver and the beauty and harmony of her life. Within her loom, she reveals her universe—light and dark, earth and sky, positive and negative. This is the soul of Navajo weaving.

Although diminishing, there is a core of weavers that still endures with vitality, vision and innovation.

Shiprock Trading Company, Shiprock, New Mexico
Red Rock Trading Post, Red Valley, Arizona
Shonto Trading Post, Shonto, Arizona

Steve Simpson
TRADER

Navajo rugs have been part of my life as long as I can remember. When I was young, as a result of my father's love of the trading business, we often had rugs layered three deep on the floor of our home in Bluff, Utah. Although I do not specifically remember the patterns, sizes or who wove the rugs, I certainly remember the warmth they brought to the house. The deep reds of the Ganado patterns, and the soft earth tones of the Two Grey Hills weaving have stayed in my memory, even though the rugs have long since been sold or traded to new owners. I also remember the Indian traders of that era telling me that Navajo rugs would no longer be made by the time I reached their age. The implication was that Navajo weaving was a dying art.

My father, William W. "Duke" Simpson, had always wanted to open a trading post in Bluff. His dream was realized when Twin Rocks Trading Post opened in the summer of 1989. By that time, I was aware of the history of Navajo weaving, and had visions of influencing a new regional style. I knew of early traders such as Lorenzo Hubbell, C.N. Cotton and J.B. Moore, and how they kept Navajo weaving alive and infused it with new vitality in the late 1800s and early 1900s.

After working on the project a few years, I began to worry that the time for trading posts influencing new weaving styles had passed. The trading post era had long since ended, and contemporary traders were generally not as closely affiliated with the weavers as the old traders had been. The new mobility resulting from paved roads and readily available transportation had liberated the artists.

As we pursued our ambition, it became apparent that many of the weavers did not want to weave the same patterns over and over again. The creative floodgates had been opened, the weavers had been exposed to a variety of outside influences and they felt free to create their own personal styles. We noticed very quickly that many of these new weavings were very creative, and that this new movement was even better than what we had initially envisioned. These new patterns were frequently stunning, and generated genuine passion from the patrons visiting the trading post. Based upon this new understanding, our focus changed from attempting to influence a new regional pattern to being a catalyst for innovation.

In the late 1800s and early 1900s, Hubbell, Cotton and Moore were responsible for moving Navajo weaving in new directions; ultimately reviving and reinvigorating the art. It is generally accepted that in doing so these traders saved the craft from extinction. Today, traders such as Bruce Burnham, Steve Getzwiller and Mark Winter are following in their footsteps. As a result of their work with, and love of the people, the future of Navajo weaving seems secure. We are happy to be part of the process, and hope the Navajo weaving tradition endures for our children and grandchildren.

Twin Rocks Trading Post—Bluff, Utah

Virginia & Bruce Burnham
TRADER

I began my trading career in 1960 as a 20-year-old "green" store clerk at Redrock Trading Post near the Arizona/New Mexico line. I am the fourth generation of my family to do business with the Navajo Indians. My great grandfather, George Franklin Burnham, traded on the reservation out of his wagon. Grandfather, Roy Barton Burnham, built the Burnham Trading Post just east of Newcomb, New Mexico. Bisti Trading Post, south of Farmington belonged to my father, Roy Burton Burnham. I am Roy "Bruce" Burnham III and I guess trading is in my blood.

By 1970, I was at the Dennebito Trading Post and had fulfilled a vow to myself to learn the Navajo language. I had also learned so much more—the culture of these beautiful people. The truest friends I have are Navajo and with that comes the moral responsibility for their welfare. They have a deep-rooted obligation to their families, clans, friends and all human beings. In understanding the language, I began to think like a Navajo. It is much harder to say no when speaking in their tongue. Their language is pure, almost prayer-like—you can not curse if you are thinking in Navajo. I have such great appreciation for the tolerance of these people with my blundering ways and their patience in dealing with me. There is nothing that warms your heart more than a little old Navajo lady who takes your hands in hers and says "Shi Yazz" (my son). It is like a gentle caress.

It was also in 1970 that I met a beautiful Navajo woman who consented to be my wife. Virginia and I moved to Sanders, Arizona, that same year and together have operated the Burnham Trading Post ever since. We have six children and 11 grandchildren and we live in Gallup, New Mexico. Hopefully, one of our children will continue our trading heritage—the fifth generation of Burnham traders.

My chief concern for the Navajo Nation is the loss of cultural identity and values that comes with the loss of their native language. When they cease to speak Navajo, the old values and work ethics disappear also. This was the "Navajo Social Security". The dominant society will take over and with it dependency on welfare, too much red tape and corruption. The trader must continue to work hard to elevate the arts and crafts markets, encourage free enterprise on the reservation and help provide opportunities for Navajos to make a living for themselves.

The trader by decades:
1st decade, the trader is primarily concerned with making and retaining a profit;
2nd decade, the trader lightens up, is easier to deal with, and has developed a strong sense of belonging to the community
3rd decade, the trader becomes more involved in service and compassion for the community and thinks less of profit
4th decade, the trader realizes that he isn't going to be wealthy and begins to give more back to the community
5th decade, the trader is broke, but happy. He has valued customers from 2 to 40 years old who call him "shi chei" (Grandfather), a way of showing great respect. After all, who do you revere more than your grandfather? The trader has "gone native."
R.B. Burnham & Co.—Sanders, Arizona

Mark Winter

TRADER

I first encountered Native American art during the late 1960s when I was living in Southern California. I was overwhelmed by the ingenuity and integrity expressed in the art. I viewed Native American arts from the perspective of a craftsperson, and I was particularly drawn to the pattern and color relationships evident in Navajo textiles. I purchased a small collection of antique Navajo rugs in 1970, and my quest for knowledge about them was launched. Immediately my time became consumed with seeking out examples to add to my "collection."

Dealing in these wonderful textiles just "sort of" happened before I knew it. By 1975, as my collection grew, I relocated to Pagosa Springs, Colorado to expand my habit and vocation. Meeting and working with the late H. Jackson Clark and the late Dr. Joe Ben Wheat greatly enhanced my access to public and private textile collections and more accurate information about them. In 1980, I curated Jackson's and my combined collections in our first major museum exhibition. During the next 20 years the "Durango Collection" was displayed nationally to great acclaim.

By the early to mid 1990s I had decided to utilize my researching, collecting, curating, dealing, gallery and museum talents and contacts to the benefit of the historic and contemporary tradition of the Toadlena/Two Grey Hills region weavers. I realized that the beauty and integrity of the historic textiles I really loved still survived in the hearts and on the looms of the traditional weavers in this isolated portion of the Navajo Reservation.

In 1997, my wife Lerin and I purchased the Historic Toadlena Trading Post, the primary trading post in the area and restored it to reflect its origins. We created the Two Grey Hills Weaving Museum to honor the achievements of the past and present local weavers. We currently (September 2002) are showing our 4th major exhibit at the museum, titled Dances With Wool.

I feel I might be one of the luckiest people ever to appreciate Navajo textiles. I have gained a deep insight into the historical roots of the tradition, and at the same time, have established very close relationships with some of the best living Navajo weavers. What I most appreciate about the weavers from our region is that in the 21st century they still retain a closeness to the traditional process. They raise their own sheep and shear their own wool. They wash, card, comb and spin their own yarns. They weave incredible designs without any pre-patterns on the same looms their great grandmothers used.

Different people may like different patterns and colors, but technically speaking, the textiles created by the Toadlena/Two Grey Hills weavers are unsurpassed anywhere on the entire reservation today. The daily experiences of getting to know, and being able to work with these Native American artists, has enriched my life beyond measure.

I invite all interested people to come to Toadlena and experience the tradition that Lorenzo Hubble lamented more than 100 years ago was destined to quickly pass. Thankfully, the tradition lives on, as all great traditions should.

Toadlena Trading Post—Newcomb, New Mexico

Regional Weaving Styles

Chinle • Yeibichai • Teec nos Pos • Two Grey Hills • Sand Painting • Crystal • Burntwater • Pine Springs
Klagetoh • Pine Springs • Wide Ruins • Ganado • Storm • Pictorial • Raised Outline • Saddle Blankets • Two Faced/Twill

Acknowledgments

We sincerely appreciate the support and help of the following traders:
Bruce and Virginia Burnham, R.B. Burnham & Co. Trading Post, Sanders, Arizona
Mark Winter, Toadlena Trading Post, Chuck and Phyllis Kinsey Mgrs, Toadlena, New Mexico
Bill Malone and Brenda Spencer, Hubbell Trading Post, Ganado, Arizona
Steve Simpson, Twin Rocks Trading Post, Bluff, Utah
Jed Foutz, Shiprock Trading Post, Shiprock, Arizona

Janet Walkup, Gladys Northrup and Jolene Campbell for their editing.

We wish to thank the following for their consideration with accommodations for our project.
The Navajo Nation Inn, Window Rock, Arizona
Holiday Inn, Canyon De Chelly, Chinle, Arizona
Desert Rose Inn, Bluff, Utah
Best Western Chieftain, Chambers, Arizona

To our families and many friends for their encouragement to complete this book.
To the Navajo Nation, Department of Tourism, Fred White, Director, Window Rock, AZ.

To the Navajo Weavers, the beautiful gentle people that opened their homes and hearts to us.
We proudly call you friends.
May you always walk in beauty.

Glossary

ARRANGED MARRIAGE Family of the groom usually calls on the bride's family to arrange terms of the relationship, couple may not know each other.

BARTER/TRADE Business without the exchange of money.

BATTEN Smooth flat wood tool used to keep shed open while weft is inserted.

CARD To comb and clean wool by pulling it between the teeth of metal carding tools.

CEREMONIALS/SINGS Navajo rituals performed by a medicine man or singer to heal or protect a person. (i.e. Blessing Way, Beauty Way, Enemy Way, etc.)

CHAPTER HOUSE Navajo Town Hall type government in village areas.

CLAN Multigenerational groups of common identity, organization, and property that descends from a common ancestor. Marriage within clan is strictly prohibited.

DINE' Navajo word meaning, "The People" Navajos often refer to themselves as Dine'.

DREAMCATCHERS Small hoop-shaped webbed ornaments with beads and feathers; catches bad dreams when hung over bed. Good dreams filter through.

DYEING To color wool by soaking it in a hot solution of vegetal material.

GRANDMOTHER A term of endearment for a revered elderly woman.

HOZHO Navajo word meaning beauty, harmony and happiness.

HOGAN Traditional Navajo dwelling containing six or eight sides, made of logs, stone or wood and covered with mud. Roof may be cone (Male) or dome (Female) shaped with a smoke hole in the center. Doorways always face east.

LEARN PAPER Early Navajo term for going to school.

MUTUAL HOUSES Low-cost housing provided to the Navajo on a rent to own basis, located close to public schools for convenience of childrens' education.

NALI Grandmother on Father's Side.

OUTFIT/COMPOUND/HOME SITE LEASE Land leased by Navajo government to a family which may contain homes of several generations.

POW WOW Navajo gathering for dances and socializing.

PUT A RUG UP String warp under tension on an upright loom to begin a rug.

RUG ROOM A room in a trading post to display rugs for sale or as a museum setting.

REGIONAL WEAVING STYLES Patterns named after the various reservation areas where they began. In today's mobile society a weaver may use many patterns.

SANDPAINTINGS/DRYPAINTINGS Pictures created for Navajo ceremonies by a medicine man using colored sand and pollen for his pallete. To cure and restore harmony to patients. Destroyed after ceremony.

SHADE/BRUSH RAMADA Open structure for shade created from branches and wooden poles for outdoor living.

SHEEP CAMP Land used for grazing flocks of sheep away from main dwellings.

SHED Opening between front and back warps into which weft is inserted.

SPIDER WOMAN Legendary woman who lived in Spider Rock in Canyon de Chelly and taught the Navajo to weave.

SPINNING Navajos use the stick-and-whorl spindle method twirling the shaft with the right hand and drawing the fibers from a pad of carded wool fastened to the tip of the spindle shaft and twisted together as it revolves.

SPIRIT TRAIL/WEAVERS PATH/DOORWAY A thin line of light-colored weft woven from the center design area through the borders to the outer edge of the rug at an upper corner; allows the creative spirit to escape.

TAPESTRY Weaving containing 80 to over 120 wefts per inch. Most time-consuming and most expensive.

THE LONG WALK A grueling winter forced walk of more than 300 miles to Bosque Redondo, NM, made by 8,000 Navajos after they were conquered in 1863-1864. Allowed to return to their homeland between the four sacred mountains in 1868.

WARP A fine tightly spun yarn tied onto the loom under tension before weaving starts.

WEAVING COMB Wooden comb used to tap the weft wool tightly into place.

WEFT Softly spun yarn that is woven over and under warp from one side of the weaving to the other.

WINDOW ROCK, AZ Home of the Navajo Nation Council and all branches of tribal government.

YEIBICHAI Human personification of Navajo Holy People, usually dancers.

YEI Holy People, Supernatural beings.

For Further Information

Bennett, Noel and Bighorse, Tiana
1997 *Navajo Weaving Way, The Path from Fleece to Rug*
(Loveland CO: Interweave Press, Inc.)

Dedera, Don
1996 *Navajo Rugs, How to Find, Evaluate, Buy and Care for Them*
(Flagstaff, AZ: Northland Press)

Eddington, Patrick and Makov, Susan
1995 *Trading Post Guide Book*
(Flagstaff AZ: Northland Publishing Co.)

Getzwiller, Steve
1984 *The Fine Art of Navajo Weaving*
(Tucson, AZ: Ray Manley Publications)

Iverson, Peter
1990 *The Navajos*
(New York and Philadelphia: Chelsea House Publishers)

Kent, Kate Peck
1985 *Navajo Weaving: Three Centuries of Change*
(Santa Fe, NM: School of American Research Press)

Kosik, Fran
1996 *Native Roads, Self Guided Tours*
(Tucson, AZ: Rio Nuevo Publishers)

Kluckholm, Clyde and Leighton, Dorothea
2001 *The Navaho, Revised Edition*
(Cambridge, MA and London, England:
Harvard University Press)

Locks, Raymond Friday
2001 *The Book of the Navajo*, 6th Edition
(Los Angeles, CA: Mankind Publishing Co.)

Reichard, Gladys
1994 Spiderwoman
(Glorieta, NM: Rio Grande Press, Inc.)

Underhill, Ruth M.
1956 *The Navajos*
(Norman, OK: University of Oklahoma Press)